DEDICATED IN MEMORY OF MY FATHER SGT. NELSON UTLEY & THE CONTRIBUTION OF AFRICAN-AMERICAN MEN & WOMEN WHO SERVED IN WWII

To my readers,

Every single day, we African Americans are losing more and more of our history as those blacks who served are fewer and fewer in numbers, and they can no longer share their stories either by choice or by the effects of old age. We are all too familiar with, and reminded of, traditional American history and the lack of color incorporated within our history books and movies. I wanted to give back to the black community and assure them that they are not forgotten, and if I had any say so, I would not allow the upcoming generations to allow such memories to slip away.

Booker T. Washington once said, "Success is to be measured not so much by the position that one has reached in life as by the obstacles which he has overcome while trying to succeed." What better way to do that than to go back in time and tell a story of how we as a race overcame every obstacle, how we overcame every doubt, and how we fought knowing we would not make it into the history books. But because we are a people of faith, we fought and continue to fight for a country who never fought for us. Philip Randolph, a leader in the civil rights movement said it best, "Freedom is never given; it is won."

"Memorials are not just about a frozen past, but they are also about what we choose to honor in our present." – Unknown

> "Memorials are not just about a frozen past, but they are also about what we choose to honor in our present."
>
> – Unknown

Sincerely,

Richard Utley

Richard Utley

Founder/Publisher
Richard Utley
Marsha Blessing

Editor
Bill Chambrés

Managing Editor
Susan Eileen Paton

Creative Services
ZumaCreative

Mailing Address
PO Box 188, Grantham, PA 17027
717-731-1405   717-427-1525 (FAX)

My War Too is published by Orison Publishers, Inc.

Connect with us

©2017 Orison Publishers, Inc. and Utley Associates. All rights reserved. No part of this issue may be reproduced by any means without prior written permission of the publisher.

Submission of text and images gives My War Too the right to edit, publish and republish them in any form or medium.

Unsolicited articles are welcome.

Front Cover photos are used from the National Archives.

www.BlacksinWWII.com
Printed in the USA

CONTENTS

ARMY'S LAST HORSE-MOUNTED UNIT
2ND CAVALRY DIVISION, 4TH CAVALRY BRIGADE 5

SHARECROPPER'S SON RECEIVES THE NAVY CROSS
STORY OF DORIS "DORIE" MILLER 6

SNAPSHOT OF THE JOURNEY FOR 19,929
AFRICAN AMERICAN MEDICS IN WWII 8

SPECIAL - ONE STUDY IN VALOR 9

SPECIAL – USS MASON AND PC-1264 9

TEN PERCENTERS
AFRICAN-AMERICAN WOMEN IN THE WOMEN'S ARMY AUXILIARY CORP 10

RED BALL EXPRESS 13

BLOOD DRIVE LED BY A NEGRO SURGEON SAVED THEIR LIVES
DR. CHARLES R. DREW AND NATIONAL BLOOD DRIVES 14

HOMEFRONT FOR AFRICAN AMERICANS 16

OBSERVER BECOMES PILOT
STORY OF RAYMOND N. TRIPLETT 18

SPECIAL – BLUE HELMETS OF THE 93RD INFANTRY DIVISION 19

"BLACK PANTHERS" OF THE 761ST TANK BATTALION
OUTNUMBERED AND OUTGUNNED 20

USS HARMON
1ST NAVY SHIP NAMED AFTER AN AFRICAN AMERICAN 23

WORLD WAR II'S "BUFFALO SOLDIERS"
92ND INFANTRY DIVISION 24

AFRICAN-AMERICAN TROOPS AND THE 'ALCAN' HIGHWAY 26

TUSKEGEE AIRMEN
99TH PURSUIT SQUADRON 29

FROM MONTFORD POINT TO IWO JIMA
ONE PATH FOR AFRICAN AMERICAN MARINES IN WWII 30

FROM THE EDITOR:

This 32-page journal-type magazine is not intended, by any degree, to be a complete history of the dedicated services of the millions of African-American men and women who served in World War II. It is instead a birds-eye view of some of these patriots and the units with which they served. It is also intended as an encouragement for readers to explore the complete histories and contributions of their participation in the war. A starting point might be, for example, the history of the 92nd Infantry Division.

THIS PUBLICATION IS DEDICATED TO THE MEMORY OF ALL THOSE THAT SERVED, WHETHER ABROAD OR AT HOME.

About the Editor

It was with the 150th anniversary of the Civil War that Bill Chambrés began to write a series that would cover the important battles of that conflict. However, as a run-up to that series, he wrote over 70 blogs covering the history and politics of America during the period 1830 to 1861. It was titled *Footsteps to a War*.

His Civil War battle coverage was based upon the Civil War Sites Advisory Committee's report to Congress in 1993. That report sited 384 battles that they considered the most important using four distinct categories. He then compiled a review of each of these battles, each of which was released as a blog on the exact date the battle was fought 150 years previously. This project took exactly the same number of days as the war itself.

He followed this with a 24-chapter series he considered a natural follow-up to the war. That series was simply titled *Reconstruction*. Because of its complexity, he considers that series the most difficult he has ever written.

When he was approached by long-time friend and associate Richard H. Utley to edit a brief series of accomplishments and contributions of African-American men and women during World War II, he accepted the opportunity. What you will find in the enclosed pages of this journal is by no means the entire story, nor is it intended to be. However, hopefully, as readers you will dig deeper into any of these episodes that push your history button for more knowledge.

William Chambrés is a member of the American Historical Association, the Company of Military Historians, the Organization of American Historians, and the Society for Military History. He is the Historian Laureate for Cheltenham, Pennsylvania, and the editor of the website, www.historic-lamott-pa.com. ★

THE ARMY'S LAST HORSE-MOUNTED UNIT:

THE 2ND CAVALRY DIVISION, 4TH CAVALRY BRIGADE. BY: BILL CHAMBRÉS

The 2nd Cavalry Division, 4th Cavalry brigade was activated February 21, 1941, and was considered one of the outstanding African-American fighting units during World War II, a designation they shared with such other notable units as the 92nd Infantry Division, 366th Infantry Regiment; the 93rd Infantry Division, 369th Infantry Regiment; and the 332d Fighter Group (Tuskegee Airmen).

The 2nd Cav, the army's last horse-mounted unit, was activated under command of Major General Harry H. Johnson at Fort Clark near Brackettville, Texas. Mobilized for deployment to North Africa on January 12, 1944, the unit was inactivated in Oran, Algeria, on March 9, 1944.

In all, more than 10,000 African-American cavalrymen served during World War II. But, even prior to the war, the modern history of African Americans in the cavalry is tangled and somewhat difficult to follow. The 4th Cavalry Brigade (Colored) which included a Weapons Troop (Colored), and the 9th Cavalry Regiment (Colored) was reassigned in October of 1940. Also in the Brigade was the 10th Cavalry Regiment (Colored) which was originally activated on March 24, 1923. The Regiment was later transferred to the 3rd Cavalry Division on August 15, 1927, and then to the 2nd Cavalry Division on October 10, 1940.

After the Army decided to dismount the cavalry, they were uncertain as to what they should do with these troops. The February 25, 1943, activation of the 2nd Cavalry allowed African-American enlisted personnel to be trained as a combat division. However, despite the need for more combat troops in Italy, after the 2nd Cavalry began to disembark in Oran, Algeria, on March 4, 1944, the division was inactivated, and its troops were used to create support and service units. One small contingent of African-American cavalrymen retained their horses throughout the war but did so only to train white officer cadets at the U.S. Military Academy.

Another small number of black cavalrymen traded in their horses for armored cars and saw combat in Italy and the Pacific Theater, as the division reconnaissance troops of the 92nd and 93rd Infantry Divisions.

The 10th Cavalry regiment, which had been folded into the 4th Brigade of the 2nd Cavalry Division, saw no action in World War II and was deactivated in North Africa in May 1944 with its personnel transferred to other service units. ★

A SHARECROPPER'S SON RECEIVES THE NAVY CROSS

THE STORY OF DORIS "DORIE" MILLER. BY: BILL CHAMBRÉS

The Japanese fighter plane attack on Pearl Harbor, just before 8 a.m. on December 7, 1941, produced the first African-American hero of World War II.

Doris "Dorie" Miller had been born in Waco, Texas, to Connery Miller, a sharecropper, and his wife Henrietta. He was the third of four sons and helped around the house, cooking meals and doing laundry, as well as working on the family farm. Miller was a good student and was a fullback on the football team at Waco's A.J. Moore High School.

On September 16, 1939, he enlisted in the United States Navy to help support his family with his monthly pay of $50. He became a Mess Attendant, Third Class, one of the few positions then open to African Americans. Following training at the Naval Training Station in Norfolk, Virginia, he was assigned to the ammunition ship Pyro, but on January 2, 1940, was transferred to the battleship West Virginia, where he became the main cook.

In the U.S. Navy of 1941, the only duties available to African Americans were those of mess attendant and cook. They were forbidden to practice with or fire any type of weapon, and their assigned battle stations were as ammunition handlers. All meals and accommodations were segregated.

REPRODUCTION NO: 208-PMP-68; ABOVE AND BEYOND THE CALL OF DUTY. COLOR POSTER OF DORIS (DORIE) MILLER BY DAVID STONE MARTIN. 1943.

On that fateful Sunday morning Miller was collecting laundry in the bowels of the battleship USS West Virginia. His other duties for the day were to serve and clear the tables in the junior officers' mess, shine shoes, and make the beds. But that all changed when the alarm for General Quarters sounded throughout the twenty-year-old ship.

The then 22-year-old Miller ran to his battle station at the antiaircraft battery magazine amidships. As the West Virginia shuddered and listed from three portside torpedo blasts, he found the magazine too damaged to use and made his way to the deck following pre-planned orders. Once there he reported himself available for other duty. Lieutenant Commander Doir C. Johnson, the ship's communications officer, ordered Miller to help him move the ship's captain, Mervyn Bennion, who had a severe shrapnel wound in his abdomen. They moved the captain from the damaged bridge to a sheltered spot behind the conning tower where the captain, who refused to leave his post, questioned his officers about the condition of the ship and gave orders.

Miller, under Lt. Frederic H. White's orders, began loading the unmanned #1 and #2 Browning .50 caliber anti-aircraft machine guns aft of the conning tower. Miller was not familiar with the machine gun, but White and Ensign Delano told him what to do. Miller had served both men as a room steward and knew them well. Although Delano only expected Miller to feed ammunition to one gun, Miller began firing.

Miller fired the gun until he ran out of ammunition, at which time he was ordered by other officers to carry the captain up to the navigation bridge out of the thick smoke caused by the many fires onboard the ship. Captain Bennion was only partially conscious at this point and died soon afterwards. Japanese aircraft would eventually drop two armor-piercing bombs through the deck of the battleship and launch five 18 in (460 mm) aircraft torpedoes into her port side. When the attack finally lessened, Miller helped move injured sailors through oil and water to the quarterdeck, thereby "unquestionably saving the lives of a number of people who might otherwise have been lost."

The ship was heavily damaged by bombs, torpedoes, and resulting explosions and fires, but the crew prevented her from capsizing by counter-flooding a number of compartments. Instead, the West Virginia sank to the harbor bottom as her surviving crew, including Miller, abandoned ship.

Dorie Miller's brave actions during the attack on Pearl Harbor made him the first African American to be awarded the Navy Cross, the second highest military decoration that may be awarded to a member of the US Navy or Marine Corps, for extraordinary heroism.

On December 13, 1941, Miller reported to USS Indianapolis and then returned to the west coast of the United States in November 1942. Assigned to the newly constructed USS Liscome Bay in the spring of 1943, Miller was on board that escort carrier during Operation Galvanic, the seizure of Makin and Tarawa Atolls in the Gilbert Islands.

At 5:10 a.m. on November 24th, while cruising near Butaritari Island, a single torpedo from a Japanese submarine struck the escort carrier near the stern. The aircraft bomb magazine detonated a few moments later, sinking the warship within minutes. Listed as missing following the loss of the escort carrier was Cook Third Class Dorie Miller. He was officially presumed dead November 25, 1944, a year and a day after the loss of the ship. In all, 646 sailors died as a result of the sinking of Liscome Bay, with 272 surviving.

In addition to the Navy Cross, Miller was entitled to the Purple Heart Medal, the American Defense Service Medal, Fleet Clasp, the Asiatic-Pacific Campaign Medal, and the World War II Victory Medal. But perhaps the greatest honor of all was when, on June 30, 1973, the USS Miller was commissioned. The Miller is a Knox-class destroyer escort in the United States Navy and is named in honor of Cook Third Class Doris "Dorie" Miller. ★

RESCUING SURVIVORS NEAR THE USS WEST VIRGINIA AFTER THE ATTACK ON PEARL HARBOR, DECEMBER 7, 1941. IMAGE 80-G-19930. U.S. NAVAL HISTORY AND HERITAGE COMMAND PHOTOGRAPH.

REPRODUCTION NO: 208-PMP-68; "ADMIRAL C. W. NIMITZ, CINCPAC, PINS NAVY CROSS ON DORIS MILLER, AT CEREMONY ON BOARD WARSHIP IN PEARL HARBOR, T. H." MAY 27, 1942.

SNAPSHOT OF THE JOURNEY FOR 19,929

AFRICAN AMERICAN MEDICS IN WWII
BY: BILL CHAMBRÉS

According to records from 1944, most African Americans who were in "technical" services were in the Quartermaster or Engineering groups. But the medical services were also well represented with nearly 20,000 African Americans serving: 342 officers and 19,587 enlisted personnel.

Though some African-American doctors and nurses were sent to a few all-black hospitals or the black wards of Station Hospitals, the majority of black MDs went either into ambulance and sanitary companies or served in the Medical Detachments of segregated combat and support units. The Surgeon General was opposed to integration of African-American doctors and nurses with white professionals, therefore no other option was considered and all-black wards were established in some hospitals, such as Ft. Bragg, North Carolina and Camp Livingston, Louisiana.

By 1942 there were two all-black hospitals, in Arizona, run by the Army, and Alabama, run by the Air Corps. But after pressure from groups advocating increased use of black medical workers, the Surgeon General allowed procurement of additional African-American personnel to be more widely used on a non-segregated basis (though still under white command).

African-American nurses also faced racial segregation and discrimination. The National Association of Colored Graduate Nurses lobbied for a change in the discriminatory policies of the Army Nurse Corps. Recognizing the need for action, First Lady Eleanor Roosevelt urged the Army surgeon general to recruit African-American nurses for service and the Army complied, albeit rather unwillingly. In 1941, the Army Nurse Corps began accepting African-American nurses, though due to a quota system only a small number, 56, were allowed to join. Slowly, African-American nurses pierced the barriers within the military system. By April 1941, 48 black nurses were assigned to Camp Livingston, Louisiana and Fort Bragg, North Carolina. Della Raney Jackson, a graduate of Lincoln Hospital School of Nursing in Durham, North Carolina, became the first African-American nurse to be commissioned in the U.S. Army. She reported to duty at Fort Bragg.

By May of 1943, though 183 African-American nurses held commissions in the Army Nurse Corps, this was only 0.6% of the total strength of the Army Nurse Corps. Still, black nurses worked overseas at units across the globe including Africa, Burma, Australia, and the South Pacific. In England in 1944, 63 African-American nurses worked at a 1700-bed hospital near Manchester that cared for wounded German POWs. By the conclusion of World War II, approximately 600 African-American nurses had served. ★

> REPRODUCTION NO. 111-SC-192605-S; "U.S. ARMY NURSES, NEWLY ARRIVED, LINE THE RAIL OF THEIR VESSEL AS IT PULLS INTO PORT OF GREENOCK, SCOTLAND, IN EUROPEAN THEATER OF OPERATIONS. THEY WAIT TO DISEMBARK AS THE GANGPLANK IS LOWERED TO THE DOCK." AUGUST 15, 1944. MEYER. NATIONAL ARCHIVES AND RECORDS ADMINISTRATION.

ONE STUDY IN VALOR

WAVERLY WOODSON'S FIRST ARMY PORTRAIT. [PHOTO COURTESY OF JOANN WOODSON VIA WWW.LINDAHERVIEUX.COM]

In the early morning hours of D-Day, Philadelphia-born Corporal Waverly "Woody" D. Woodson was in a Landing Craft Tank, admiring the emerging French coastline and the cliffs over Omaha beach. He was one of five medics aboard the LCT that left England on June 5, 1944. "That beauty didn't last long when the Germans starting messing with us," he would say later. "They were shelling the devil out of us. At the same time, we went over two submerged mines. The whole thing jumped up out of the water."

Although Woodson was hit by shrapnel that passed through his leg and lodged in his groin area, he scrambled ashore and set up a makeshift aid station. It was later estimated that he treated as many as 200 wounded. At one point, a rope line broke from the shore to a stranded British landing craft. Woodson pulled four men from the water and revived them, all the while teaching those around him how to resuscitate a drowning man.

Woodson's actions were celebrated in the African-American press, which declared him the "No. 1 Invasion Hero." He eventually received the Bronze Star and Purple Heart and was recommended for the Distinguish Service Cross and then the Medal of Honor. Woodson's commander had recommended him for the Distinguished Service Cross and Gen. John C. H. Lee had upgraded the recommendation to what was then called the Congressional Medal of Honor. He also recommended that President Roosevelt might want to personally present the medal as he had done for some white soldiers.

Waverly Woodson died in 2005 without ever receiving his Medal of Honor. Despite the fact that more than one million African Americans served in World War II, not one received the Medal of Honor before 1997. An independent Army investigation in 1995 concluded that pervasive racism was to blame. On January 13, 1997, President Clinton awarded the Medal of Honor to seven African Americans. Seventeen years later, in 2014, President Barack Obama presented five more Medals of Honor to those who served during WWII. Yet still, Waverly Woodson, the 320th's Barrage Balloon undisputed hero, was not among them.

For more on this story see Linda Hervieux's new book on the 320th, Forgotten: The Untold Story of D-Day's Black Heroes, At Home and At War, published by HarperCollins.

THE USS MASON AND PC-1264

During World War II, there were two ships that had predominantly African-American crews: the USS Mason, a destroyer escort, and PC 1264, a submarine chaser. Though initially all officers and petty officers were white, the objective was to replace them with African-American officers as soon as possible. Samuel Lee Gravely became the first black officer in the Navy and was assigned to PC 1264. The goal of an African American officer staffing was never achieved on the USS Mason.

The crews' performances on both PC 1264 and the USS Mason led the U.S. Navy to reevaluate its perception of African Americans as members of the fleet. The 2004 film Proud dramatizes the story of the Mason.

COMMISSIONING CEREMONIES, 25 APRIL 1944, AT NEW YORK CITY. NOTE 40MM SINGLE GUN MOUNT BEYOND THE OFFICERS, AND READY-SERVICE RACKS FOR K-GUN DEPTH CHARGES ON EACH SIDE. U.S. NAVAL HISTORY AND HERITAGE COMMAND PHOTOGRAPH.

THE TEN PERCENTERS:
AFRICAN-AMERICAN WOMEN IN THE WOMEN'S ARMY AUXILIARY CORPS
BY: BILL CHAMBRÉS

PHOTOGRAPH NO. 111-SC-144958; "WAACS AT WORK IN TEMP. BLDG. 'M', 26TH STREET, WASHINGTON, DC, WAAC HEADQUARTERS. LEFT TO RIGHT: LTS. HARRIET WEST AND IRMA CAYTON, ...GOING OVER THEIR RECRUITING SCHEDULE REPORT." 1942. WILFRED MORGAN. NATIONAL ARCHIVES AND RECORDS ADMINISTRATION.

Early in 1941, Massachusetts Congresswoman Edith Nourse Rogers met with General George C. Marshall, the Army's Chief of Staff, and informed him that she intended to introduce a bill to establish an Army Women's Corps, separate and distinct from the existing Army Nurse Corps.

Rogers remembered the female civilians who had worked overseas with the Army under contract and as volunteers during World War I as communications specialists and dietitians. Because these women had served the Army without benefit of official status, they had to obtain their own food and quarters, and they received no legal protection or medical care. Upon their return home they were not entitled to the disability benefits or pensions available to U.S. military veterans. Rogers was determined that if women were to serve again with the Army in a wartime theater they would receive the same legal protection and benefits as their male counterparts.

As public sentiment increasingly favored the creation of some form of a women's corps, Army leaders decided to work with Rogers to devise and sponsor an organization that would constitute the least amount of threat to the Army's existing culture. Although Rogers believed the women's corps should be a part of the Army, so that women would receive equal pay, pension, and disability benefits, the Army did not want to accept women directly into its ranks.

Rogers introduced her bill in Congress in May 1941, but it failed to receive serious consideration until after the Japanese attack on Pearl Harbor in December of that year. General Marshall's active support and congressional testimony helped the Rogers bill through Congress. Marshall believed that U.S. engagement in a two-front war would cause an eventual manpower shortage. The Army could ill afford to spend the time and money necessary to train men in essential service skills such as typing and switchboard operations when highly-skilled women were already available. Marshall and others felt that women were inherently suited to certain critical communications jobs which, while repetitious, demanded high levels of manual dexterity. They believed that men tended to become impatient with such jobs and might make careless mistakes which could be costly during war.

Congressional opposition to the bill centered around some southern congressmen. With women in the armed services, one representative asked, "Who will then do the cooking, the washing, the mending, the humble homey tasks to which every woman has devoted herself; who will nurture the children?" After a long and acrimonious debate, which filled 98 columns in the Congressional Record, the bill finally passed the House 249 to 86. The Senate approved the bill 38 to 27 on May 14, 1941. When President Franklin D. Roosevelt signed the bill into law the next day, he set a recruitment goal of 25,000 for the first year. Women's Army Auxiliary Corps (WAAC) recruiting topped that goal by November, at which point Secretary of War Henry L. Stimson authorized WAAC enrollment at 150,000, the original ceiling set by Congress.

Organization of the WAAC recruiting drive and training centers began immediately. Fort Des Moines, Iowa, was selected as the site of the first WAAC training center. Applications for the WAAC officer training program were made available at Army recruiting stations on May 27, with a return deadline of June 4, 1941. Applicants for officer training had to be U.S. citizens between the ages of 21 and 45, have no dependents, be at least five feet tall, and weigh over 100 pounds (but less than 200). Over 35,000 women from all over the country applied for less than 1,000 anticipated positions.

The first officer candidate training class of 440 women started a six-week course at Fort Des Moines. Interviews conducted by an eager press revealed that the average officer candidate was 25 years old, had attended college, and was working as an office administrator, executive secretary, or teacher. One out of every five had enlisted because a male member of her family was in the armed forces and she wanted to help him get home sooner. Several were combat widows of Pearl Harbor and Bataan.

The forty black women who entered the first WAAC officer candidate class were placed in a separate platoon. Although they attended classes and mess with the other officer candidates, post facilities such as service clubs, theaters, and beauty shops were segregated. Black officer candidates had backgrounds similar to those of white officer candidates—almost 80 percent had attended college, and the majority had work experience as teachers and office workers.

In July, Army recruiting centers were supplied with applications for volunteers to enlist in the WAAC as auxiliaries (enlisted women). The response, although not as dramatic as the officer candidate applications, was still gratifying. Those who had applied unsuccessfully for officer training and who had stated on their applications that they would be willing to come in as auxiliaries did not have to reapply. Women were told that after the initial group of officers had been trained, all other officer candidates would be selected from the ranks of the auxiliaries as the corps grew. The first auxiliary class started its four-week basic training at Fort Des Moines on August 17, 1941.

PHOTOGRAPH NO. 111-SC-238651; "WAAC CAPT. CHARITY ADAMS OF COLUMBIA, NC, WHO WAS COMMISSIONED FROM THE FIRST OFFICER CANDIDATE CLASS, AND THE FIRST OF HER GROUP TO RECEIVE A COMMISSION, DRILLS HER COMPANY ON THE DRILL GROUND AT THE FIRST WAAC TRAINING CENTER, FORT DES MOINES, IOWA." MAY 1943. NATIONAL ARCHIVES AND RECORDS ADMINISTRATION.

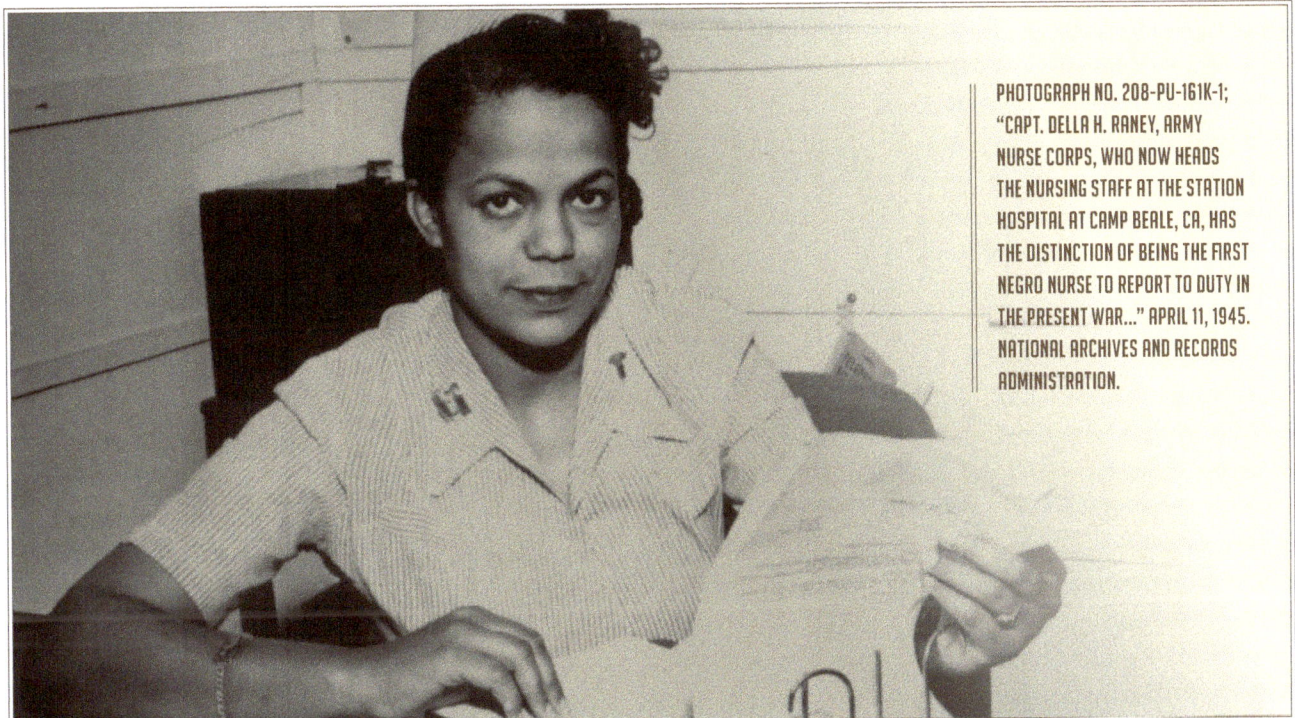

PHOTOGRAPH NO. 208-PU-161K-1; "CAPT. DELLA H. RANEY, ARMY NURSE CORPS, WHO NOW HEADS THE NURSING STAFF AT THE STATION HOSPITAL AT CAMP BEALE, CA, HAS THE DISTINCTION OF BEING THE FIRST NEGRO NURSE TO REPORT TO DUTY IN THE PRESENT WAR..." APRIL 11, 1945. NATIONAL ARCHIVES AND RECORDS ADMINISTRATION.

The first classes of both WAAC officer candidates and enlisted personnel were trained by male Regular Army officers. Col. Donald C. Faith was chosen to command the center. Faith's background as an educator and his interest in the psychology of military education rendered him well suited for his position.

Eventually, and gradually, WAAC officers took over the training of the rest of the corps. The majority of the newly trained WAAC officers, the first of whom finished their training on August 29, were assigned to Fort Des Moines, Iowa, to conduct basic training. As officer classes continued to graduate throughout the fall of 1942, many were assigned to staff three new WAAC training centers in Daytona Beach, Florida; Fort Oglethorpe, Georgia; and Fort Devens, Massachusetts. Others accompanied WAAC companies sent to U.S. Army field installations across the country. Black officers were assigned to black auxiliary and officer candidate units at Fort Des Moines and Fort Devens.

Violet Hill was one of the women who completed officer training in 1942. Later in the war, Hill served as a captain and commander of Company D, 6888th Central Postal Directory Battalion.

Soldiers of the 6888th began to arrive in England on February 15, 1945. The only African-American Women's Army Corps unit sent to Europe during World War II, the 6888th was responsible for clearing years' worth of backlogged mail in both England and France. Viewing their jobs as crucial to morale at the front, they processed some 65,000 pieces of mail a shift and worked three shifts a day. At the same time, the soldiers faced constant prejudice and broke gender and racial barriers.

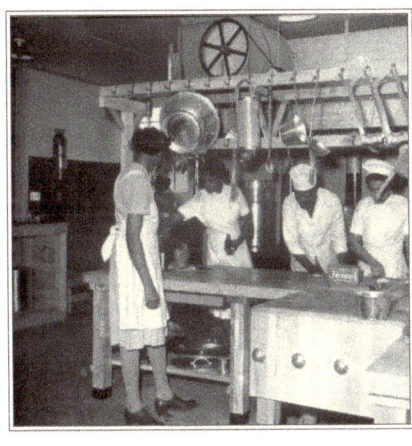

PHOTOGRAPH NO. 111-SC-162454; "... WAAC COOKS PREPARE DINNER FOR THE FIRST TIME IN NEW KITCHEN AT FORT HUACHUCA, ARIZONA." DECEMBER 5, 1942. OSTER. NATIONAL ARCHIVES AND RECORDS ADMINISTRATION.

More than 6,200 black women served with distinction in the Women's Auxiliary Army Corps. They were labeled as "ten percenters" because they made up 10 percent of the women recruited. ★

THE RED BALL EXPRESS

BY: BILL CHAMBRÉS

After Normandy, in July 1944, an acute shortage of supplies on both fronts governed all operations. With some 28 divisions advancing across France and Belgium, each requiring over 700 tons of supplies a day, Patton's 3rd Army was soon grinding to a halt from lack of fuel and ordnance. The key to pursuit lay in continuous supplies; enter the Red Ball Express.

Though the Red Ball Express only lasted three months—from August to November 1944—without it the European campaign could have dragged on for years. At its peak, the Red Ball was running 5,938 vehicles a day, each carrying 12,342 tons of supplies over a treacherous 700-mile route—marked with red balls so the drivers wouldn't get lost—often under fire. But, at the onset, there were not enough trucks or drivers, so the Army raided available units with trucks, and soldiers with non-critical duties were asked—or tasked—to become drivers. Over 75 percent of the 23,000 Red Ball Express drivers and mechanics would be African American.

A RED BALL EXPRESS TRUCK GETS STUCK IN THE MUD DURING WORLD WAR II. PHOTO COURTESY ARMY TRANSPORTATION MUSEUM.

Though only in operation for 81 days, the Red Ball Express became a legend in U.S. Army annals and American folklore, a remarkable and unparalleled, logistical achievement. As African Americans represented less than 10 percent of military personnel and were usually relegated to the Transportation Corps or other service units, their service to the Allied victory as Red Ball drivers became a point of pride for many. ★

A TRUCK DRIVER PUTS AIR INTO A TIRE ALONG THE RED BALL EXPRESS HIGHWAY. (ARMY TRANSPORTATION MUSEUM)

AFRICAN AMERICAN MEMBERS OF THE WORLD WAR II RED BALL EXPRESS REPAIR A 2.5-TON TRUCK WHILE A CREWMAN AT A MACHINE GUN KEEPS WATCH FOR THE ENEMY. PHOTO COURTESY ARMY TRANSPORTATION MUSEUM.

BLOOD DRIVE LED BY A NEGRO SURGEON SAVED THEIR LIVES:

DR. CHARLES R. DREW AND NATIONAL BLOOD DRIVES.

BY: BILL CHAMBRÉS

DR. CHARLES R. DREW

When America entered WWII, the American Red Cross announced a nationwide blood drive to build up supplies for the military. African Americans lined up to donate their blood along with other citizens but were turned away. Headlines such as "American Red Cross Bans Negro Blood!" appeared across the nation, and the Red Cross found itself in the middle of a civil rights battle.

In response to the furor, American Red Cross chairman Norman H. Davis met with the Surgeons General of the Army and Navy to work out a new blood drive policy. But this policy, approved on 1942, added to the controversy. African-American blood would be accepted, but it was to be processed and dispensed separately—in line with the Jim Crow doctrine of "separate but equal" and the belief that many wanted "plasma from blood of their own race."

The Chicago Defender would later report, after Pearl Harbor, that the first collection center for the troops set by the Red Cross in New York City was supervised by a black surgeon. Thus, they noted, "When the Japanese bombed Pearl Harbor and maimed hundreds of American soldiers and sailors, it was blood collected by a Negro surgeon that saved their lives."

That African-American surgeon was Charles R. Drew. Besides organizing America's first large-scale blood bank, he trained a generation of black physicians at Howard University. Drew was born in Washington, DC, in 1904, the son of a carpet layer (and only non-white member of the Carpet, Linoleum, and Soft-Tile Layers Union). His mother had received a teaching degree from the Miner Normal School.

Drew attended Amherst College in Massachusetts on an athletic scholarship and excelled in both track and football. He then worked as athletic director and biology and chemistry instructor at Baltimore's Morgan College (now Morgan State University). Though Drew was accepted to Harvard Medical School, he chose McGill University in Montréal, as it had a better reputation for minority treatment.

At Montréal General Hospital from 1933-1935, Drew worked closely with bacteriology professor John Beattie who was working on ways to treat shock with transfusions and other fluid replacement—this work would later lead Drew to his blood bank research. Though Drew hoped for a surgical residency at the Mayo Clinic, most major American medical centers rarely took on African-American residents. He became a pathology instructor at Howard University College of Medicine in 1935. Drew went on to Columbia University and worked

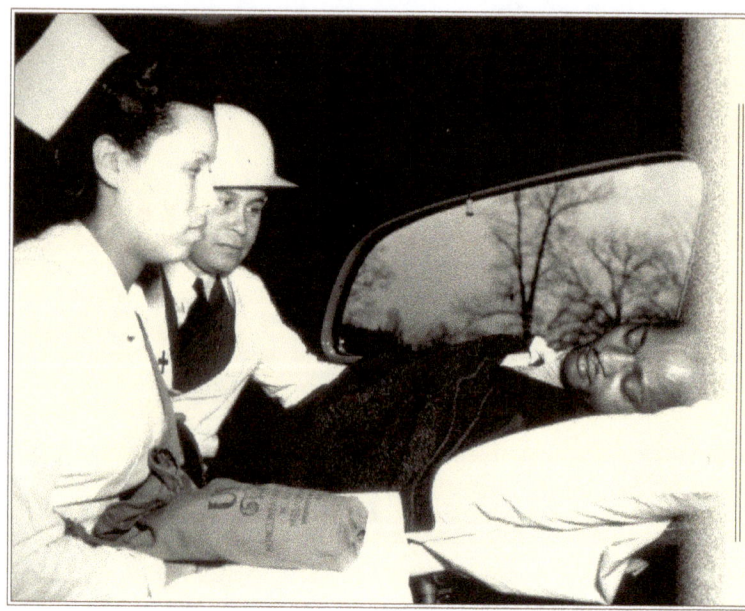

REPRODUCTION NO. 208-NP-4W-2; "AFTER RECEIVING FIRST AID TREATMENT IN PRACTICE RAID IN WASHINGTON, DC, AIR-RAID 'VICTIM' IS REMOVED TO HOSPITAL BY A MEDICAL CORPS OF THE OFFICE OF CIVILIAN DEFENSE." THE PHYSICIAN IS DR. CHARLES DREW. N.D. ROGER SMITH. NATIONAL ARCHIVES AND RECORDS ADMINISTRATION.

ON JUNE 3, 1981 A COMMEMORATIVE STAMP WAS ISSUED WITH THE IMAGE OF DR. DREW AS PART OF THE GREAT AMERICANS SERIES.

at Presbyterian hospital with John Scudder studying treatments relating to shock, blood chemistry, and transfusion. In 1939, he opened an experimental blood bank with Scudder at Presbyterian. Drew received his doctorate in medical science from Columbia in 1940, the first African American to do so.

Drew was called on to direct the 'Blood for Britain' project in 1940, and in New York, he headed a five-hospital collaboration to collect and ship plasma to Britain. Although others had developed basic methods for plasma use, Drew instituted uniform standards for collecting blood and processing plasma.

When that program ended in January 1941, Drew was appointed assistant director of a pilot program for a national blood banking system where he innovated the use of "bloodmobiles." This was at the same time that the armed forces were excluding donations from African Americans, meaning Drew was actually ineligible to participate in the program he helped establish. When the policy was modified to accept blood donations from blacks, but keep them segregated, Drew and others criticized it as both insulting and unscientific.

Drew returned to Howard University in 1941 and became Chief of Surgery at Freedmen's Hospital. He also became the first African American to be appointed an examiner for the American Board of Surgery. He would train and mentor for the next nine years while campaigning against the exclusion of black physicians from medical societies and the American Medical Association.

Drew died on April 1, 1950, from a car accident in Burlington, North Carolina. A persistent myth that Drew died after being denied admission to a white hospital or to a transfusion has been debunked repeatedly. ★

REPRODUCTION NO. K-HNP-15B; DREW IN LAB IN FRONT OF A MICROSCOPE. ARTIST BETSY GRAVES REYNEAU. NATIONAL ARCHIVES AND RECORDS ADMINISTRATION.

THE HOME FRONT FOR AFRICAN AMERICANS

During the war, with the expansion of manufacturing jobs and desegregation in war industries, many African Americans were able to secure better-paying employment. The lure of higher wages and other incentives, including leaving a culture long plagued by segregation and racial inequality, led many Southern African Americans to move to the North and West where war industry jobs were more plentiful. In all, over a million African Americans would leave the South and the rural Midwest in the 1940s. But all too frequently, any possibility of financial betterment was not accompanied by a gain in civil rights, including any significant integration in housing or education. And in the South, the dire situation of legally sanctified segregation and continued violence against blacks, including lynching, continued. ★

REPRODUCTION NO. 19-N-7058. "LSM VESSEL NO. 325 LAUNCHING PARTY." MRS. LULA MARTIN, CHICAGO, IL, SECOND FROM THE LEFT, WAS THE SPONSOR. AUGUST 25, 1944. NATIONAL ARCHIVES AND RECORDS ADMINISTRATION.

REPRODUCTION NO. 208-NP-3KK-1. "MAKING MODEL AIRPLANES FOR U.S. NAVY AT THE ARMSTRONG TECHNICAL HIGH SCHOOL. WASHINGTON, DC." MARCH 1942. MARJORY COLLINS. NATIONAL ARCHIVES AND RECORDS ADMINISTRATION.

REPRODUCTION NO. 80-G-23326. "PIN-UP GIRLS AT NAS SEATTLE, SPRING FORMAL DANCE. LEFT TO RIGHT: JEANNE MCIVER, HARRIET BERRY, MURIEL ALBERTI, NANCY GRANT, MALEINA BAGLEY, AND MATTI ETHRIDGE." APRIL 10, 1944. NATIONAL ARCHIVES AND RECORDS ADMINISTRATION.

FILE NAME 251. PHOTO CAPTION: REPRODUCTION NO. 208-NP-1KK-1. "THE NEGRO JANITORS OF THE PLANT MAINTENANCE DEPARTMENT IN NORTH AMERICA'S KANSAS CITY FACTORY IN V-FORMATION AS THEY START OUT ON THEIR DAILY TASKS." FEBRUARY 4, 1942. CARL CONLEY. NATIONAL ARCHIVES AND RECORDS ADMINISTRATION.

REPRODUCTION NO. 208-NP-4FFF-1. "TO LEARN HOW TO SHOP WITH POINT STAMPS, THESE YOUNGSTERS IN A FAIRFAX COUNTY, VIRGINIA, GRADE SCHOOL HAVE SET UP A PLAY STORE, COMPLETE WITH POINT VALUE TABLE AND INFORMATIONAL MATERIAL ON POINT RATIONING." N.D. ROGER SMITH. NATIONAL ARCHIVES AND RECORDS ADMINISTRATION.

OBSERVER BECOMES PILOT:
THE STORY OF RAYMOND N. TRIPLETT
BY: BILL CHAMBRÉS

The Triplett family name has long held close associations with the U.S. military, beginning with World War I. Members of the family continue to serve in various branches of the U.S. military.

One notable member was Raymond N. Triplett. In a document found among his effects, he tells us his story in his own words:

"Raymond N. Triplett, enlisted in the Medical detachment Station Hospital, United States Military Academy, West Point, New York, 14 August 1936.

January 1938, I was rated a medical technician and promoted to Private 1st Class. August 1938 . . . I was rated a surgical technician and assigned to the late Private Bowman's position as assistant to the surgeon of genito-urinary medicine. It was at this time that I made myself acquainted with the officers and men of the West Point Air Detachment. This resulted in numerous local and cross country flights for me in the amphibians that were stationed in the river and the railroad track, and to the north was the old Stewart Field where I flew in other types of Army aircraft."

Editor's Note: At the time, flight regulations required that all flights were to be accompanied by an "Observer." Triplett flew many times in that capacity, and, in the process, was unofficially taught how to fly. Many times he accompanied a pilot who lived in the Cheltenham area and thus was able to visit his relatives in La Mott, PA.

"11 February I was promoted to Sergeant . . . 26 February 1941, transferred me to the 366th Infantry, Fort Devans, Massachusetts."

Editor's Note: The 366th Infantry Regiment was an African-American unit that fought in both WW I and WW II. When they were activated in 1941, they were an all-black fighting unit, including black officers, an unprecedented event in U.S. history.

> At the time, flight regulations required that all flights were to be accompanied by an "Observer." Triplett flew many times in that capacity, and, in the process, was unofficially taught how to fly.

"March 1941 I was promoted to Staff Sergeant . . . May, 1942, I was promoted to 1st Sergeant.

Following maneuvers at Camp Atterbury, Indiana, the 366th Infantry transferred to Hampton Roads, Virginia. We boarded the USS William Mitchell, destination North Africa. From 28 March to 6 April 1944, I was assistant to the troop surgeon. The regiment and I disembarked 6 April at Casablanca. We bivouacked at this location until 18 April when we boarded 40 and 8's and started moving across the desert to the port of Orean, North Africa. There we boarded the HMS Orduna, in convoy with overhead air cover and sleeping on open deck. We sailed the Mediterranean to Napoli where we disembarked while under fire.

The regiment was assigned to the 15th Air Force, Regimental Headquarters and I was sent to the town of Sammichele, in close proximity to the headquarters of the 464th Bomb Group.

The C.O. was Col. William H. Bonner, an officer I had flown with while stationed at West Point. This chance meeting resulted in mission flights to ...."

Editor Note: End of document. The subsequent pages have not been located.

Although Raymond N. Triplett did not attend Army flight school, he nevertheless learned to fly and flew in U.S. Army military airplanes years before any formal training was offered to prospective black pilots. After his military service, Triplett flew as a licensed pilot and joined the Negro Airman International as a Chaplain. ★

THIS IS THE ONLY KNOWN PICTURE OF RAYMOND TRIPLETT THAT WE KNOW OF. THIS IMAGE ACTUALLY HUNG IN THE MESS HALL AT WEST POINT FOR QUITE SOME TIME.

THE BLUE HELMETS OF THE 93RD INFANTRY DIVISION

BY: BILL CHAMBRÉS

The nickname "Blue Helmets" originated during the First World War within the French Army after the Second Battle of the Marne. Consequently, its shoulder patch became a blue French Adrian helmet in commemoration.

Re-activated on May 15, 1942, at Fort Huachuca, Arizona, the U.S. 93rd Infantry Division was the first segregated division-size infantry unit mobilized in WWII. Commanded by white general staff officers and African-American junior officers and enlisted men, the 93rd was made up of the 369th, 368th, and 25th Infantry Regiments along with other field battalions and companies.

In late 1943, the 93rd moved westward to California for desert training exercises before departing for the South Pacific Theater in January, 1944 where they saw little combat and never fought as a whole unit.

While serving on Morotai Island, division troops subdued and captured Japanese forces stationed in the area, including Colonel Muisu Ouichi, the highest-ranking Japanese prisoner of war. After arriving in the Philippines at the end of 1945, the division headed back to the United States and was deactivated at Camp Stoneman, California, on February 3, 1946. ★

A MEMBER OF THE 93RD INFANTRY ADVANCES CAUTIOUSLY THROUGH THE JUNGLE IN JAPANESE TERRITORY OFF THE NUMA-NUMA TRAIL. THE ORIGINAL CAPTION NOTED HE WAS "AMONG THE FIRST NEGRO FOOT SOLDIERS TO GO INTO ACTION IN THE SOUTH PACIFIC THEATER." MAY 1, 1944. (NARA)

THE "BLACK PANTHERS" OF THE 761ST TANK BATTALION:

OUTNUMBERED AND OUTGUNNED.   BY: BILL CHAMBRÉS

The 761st Tank Battalion, formed in the spring of 1942 at Camp Claiborne, Louisiana, was the first African-American tank battalion to see combat in the Second World War. As was true for all African-American units of the time, the Commander of the battalion was a white officer, Lt. Colonel Paul L. Bates, who had been trained by George Patton.

Prior to 1940, assumptions about the inferiority of black soldiers as combat troops dominated military thinking. Blacks were segregated into support and service units to provide cooks, stevedores, truck drivers, orderlies, and other noncombat personnel. Only five African American commissioned officers served in the Army in 1941, three of whom were chaplains.

The Battalion trained at Camp Hood. During their training, Major Bates (later Lt. Colonel) was always out in front, training with his men—in the swamps and in the mud and in the steamy Louisiana drizzle that made the soldiers feel like they were bathing in a pot of Cajun gumbo. Morale improved. The battalion developed an esprit de corps. The men held their heads high and affected a cocky tanker's walk with their barracks caps tilted saucily to one side. Most in the Army still believed, however, that all the training was flash and polish toward no end. At the completion of their training they were rated superior by Second Army Commander Lt. General Ben Lear.

The 761st received orders for overseas movement on June 9, 1944. The orders came only three days after the Allies made the D-Day landings in Normandy. Three months later, the battalion departed from New York aboard the British troop transport Esperance Bay, landing in Britain on September 8. Initially assigned to the Ninth Army, the battalion was reassigned on October 2 to General Patton's Third Army. They became attached to the XII Corps 26th Infantry Division after landing at Omaha Beach in France on October 10, 1944, and they became known as the "Black Panther" Tank Battalion.

Fully armed, the 800-man 761st was equipped with 54 M4 Sherman tanks in three companies and a "mosquito fleet" company consisting of 15 smaller M5 Stuart tanks. The 761st dashed 400 miles across France in six days to catch up with Patton at Nicolas de Port. The Allies continued to squeeze an iron ring around Germany from every direction. It was the week before the attack on the fortress city of Metz that General Patton delivered his famous pep talk to his newest tankers.

The "big offensive" against entrenched German defenses kicked off at dawn on November 8. The 26th Infantry, with Patton's Panthers attached, would fight in the same sector where it had fought in 1918—on ground south of Chateau-Salins through Moncourt Woods. Opposing them were the German 11th and 13th Panzer Divisions.

While the fury of the opening battle rolled like thunder all along the length of the front line, a small enemy patrol crept through woodland thickets to where Colonel Paul Bates stood on the hood of his Jeep watching the fight. Submachine gun bullets splattered into the Jeep. A slug caught the colonel, knocking him, seriously wounded, to the ground. The commander the Panthers had trusted and depended on, who had developed their pride as a fighting unit, had fallen on the first day of battle.

Also during the battle, a mine detonated underneath Sergeant Ruben Rivers's tank and shredded the flesh of his leg. Medics cleaned and dressed the wound and attempted to administer morphine for pain. Rivers pushed them away and refused to be evacuated. "Captain, you're going to need me," Rivers assured the Able Company commander, Captain David Williams. "We got a job to do."

Wounded though he was, Rivers led an echelon of tanks that blazed its way into a small village blocking the approach to the important rail and communications center of Guebling. "Don't go into that town, Sergeant!" Rivers's platoon leader radioed. "It's too hot in there." "Sorry, sir," Rivers responded. "I'm already through that town."

Rivers lost a second tank the next day. He commandeered another tank and remained in the fight. That night, a medic warned the sergeant that his wounds were getting gangrene. Rivers still refused evacuation. "Tomorrow's going to be tough," he asserted. "Another day won't make any difference."

Fighting continued in and around Guebling. By dawn of the third day of battle, Rivers and his crew had destroyed at least two enemy tanks and killed over 300 Germans. Mark IV panzers and several German tank destroyers rumbled out of the fog. "I see them!" Rivers radioed. "I'll fight them!"

Outnumbered and outgunned, Rivers and Technical Sergeant Walter James moved their two Shermans from cover and fought a delaying action that allowed Americans caught in the open to withdraw and regroup. A shell finally caught

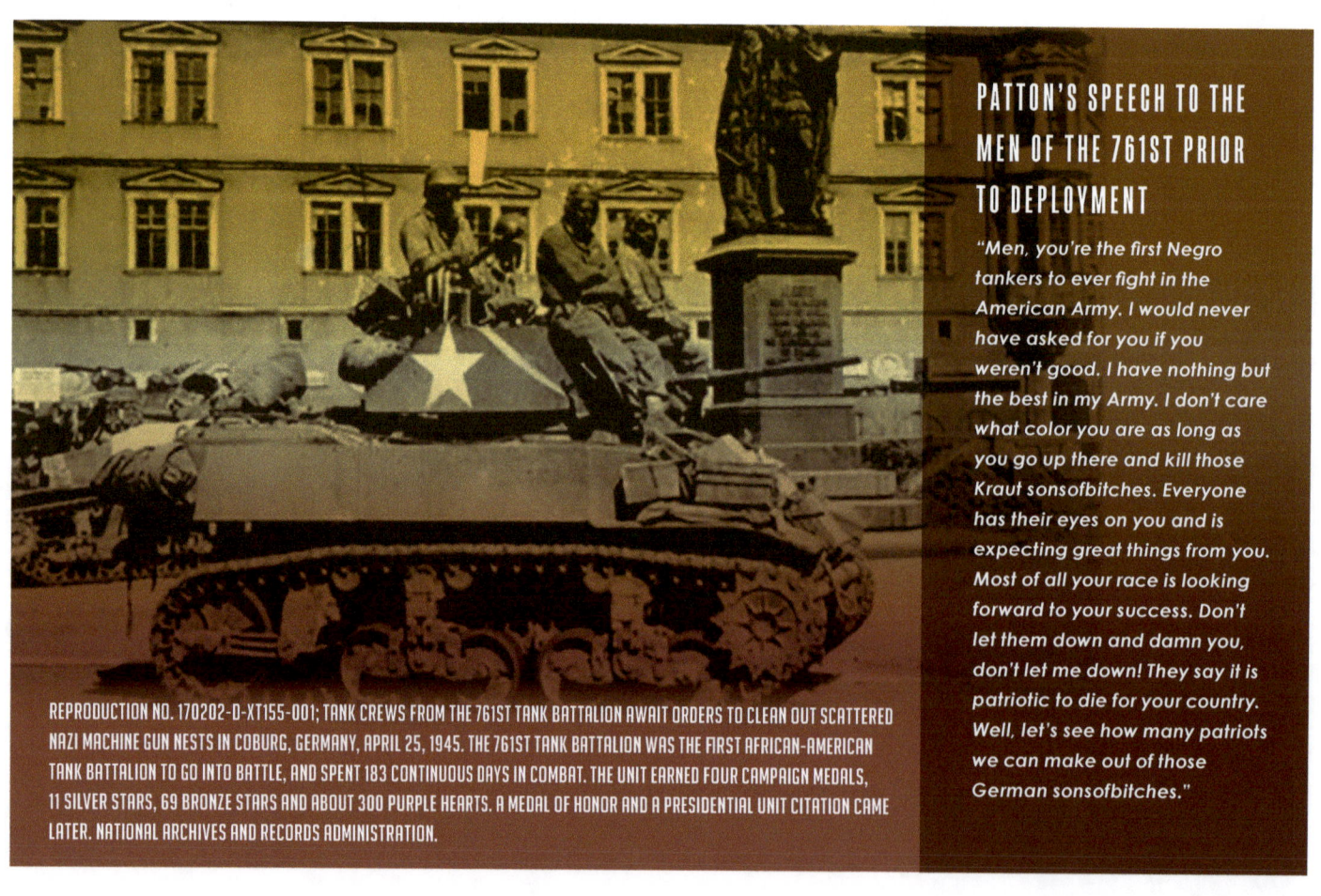

REPRODUCTION NO. 170202-D-XT155-001; TANK CREWS FROM THE 761ST TANK BATTALION AWAIT ORDERS TO CLEAN OUT SCATTERED NAZI MACHINE GUN NESTS IN COBURG, GERMANY, APRIL 25, 1945. THE 761ST TANK BATTALION WAS THE FIRST AFRICAN-AMERICAN TANK BATTALION TO GO INTO BATTLE, AND SPENT 183 CONTINUOUS DAYS IN COMBAT. THE UNIT EARNED FOUR CAMPAIGN MEDALS, 11 SILVER STARS, 69 BRONZE STARS AND ABOUT 300 PURPLE HEARTS. A MEDAL OF HONOR AND A PRESIDENTIAL UNIT CITATION CAME LATER. NATIONAL ARCHIVES AND RECORDS ADMINISTRATION.

PATTON'S SPEECH TO THE MEN OF THE 761ST PRIOR TO DEPLOYMENT

"Men, you're the first Negro tankers to ever fight in the American Army. I would never have asked for you if you weren't good. I have nothing but the best in my Army. I don't care what color you are as long as you go up there and kill those Kraut sonsofbitches. Everyone has their eyes on you and is expecting great things from you. Most of all your race is looking forward to your success. Don't let them down and damn you, don't let me down! They say it is patriotic to die for your country. Well, let's see how many patriots we can make out of those German sonsofbitches."

Rivers's tank and cracked it like an egg shell. A second armor-piercing shell finished the job. The tank commander who refused to withdraw was dead.

Colonel Bates had promised to return after being wounded during the battalion's first day of combat. He kept that promise and resumed command of the 761st on January 17. The battle-hardened battalion had changed considerably during his absence. Many of the old timers from the days at Camp Claiborne and Camp Hood were gone, some of them dead and many of them wounded. Over 30 percent of the outfit had been replaced since November.

As part of Task Force Rhine, the 761st Tank Battalion crossed that great river in March. During the fight to the last great natural barrier on the German frontier, the tankers had destroyed 31 pillboxes, 49 machine gun emplacements, 29 antitank guns, and 11 ammunition trucks. Twenty antitank guns and seven towns had been captured, while 833 Germans had been killed and 3,210 taken prisoner. Five American tanks had been lost, and 300 tons of ammunition had been expended.

On April 28, 1945, Radio Milan announced that Italian Fascist Dictator Benito Mussolini had been executed by communist guerrillas. Two days later, Hitler and his mistress, Eva Braun, committed suicide in their Berlin bunker.

The 761st Tank Battalion reached the city of Steyr, Austria, on the banks of the Enns River, on May 5, 1945. Over 100,000 German soldiers, fleeing the advancing Soviet Red Army, surrendered to American troops, who herded them into a large field that had become a makeshift holding facility.

By the end of the war, the 761st Tank Battalion had been in combat for 183 continuous days. During this time, it participated in four major Allied campaigns in six different countries and was attached to three separate American armies and seven different divisions. The Black Panthers had inflicted more than 130,000 casualties on the enemy. Doing so cost them: three officers and 31 enlisted men had been killed in action and 22 officers and 180 enlisted men had been wounded. Eight black enlisted men received battlefield commissions, while 391 received decorations for heroism, including 246 Purple Hearts, 56 Bronze Stars, 7 Silver Stars (3 of them posthumously), and one Medal of Honor awarded posthumously to Sergeant Ruben Rivers

In 1998, the 761st Tank Battalion received a much delayed Presidential Unit Citation. ★

REPRODUCTION NO. 111-SC-196106-S; "CPL. CARLTON CHAPMAN...IS A MACHINE-GUNNER IN AN M-4 TANK, ATTACHED TO A MOTOR TRANSPORT UNIT NEAR NANCY, FRANCE." 761ST MT. BN. NOVEMBER 5, 1944. RYAN. NATIONAL ARCHIVES AND RECORDS ADMINISTRATION.

THE USS HARMON:
THE 1ST NAVY SHIP NAMED AFTER AN AFRICAN AMERICAN.

BY: BILL CHAMBRÉS

POSTER FEATURING MESS ATTENDANT HARMON AND USS HARMON, NAMED IN HIS HONOR. HE WAS KILLED IN ACTION ON BOARD USS SAN FRANCISCO DURING THE BATTLE OF GUADALCANAL, 13 NOVEMBER 1942. FOR HIS HEROISM HARMON WAS POSTHUMOUSLY AWARDED THE NAVY CROSS WHICH IS ALSO PICTURED. (U.S. NAVAL HISTORY AND HERITAGE COMMAND PHOTOGRAPH)

USS HARMON TAKEN IN AUGUST 1943 WHEN THE SHIP WAS FIRST COMPLETED BUT WAS RETOUCHED BY THE CENSOR TO REMOVE RADAR ANTENNAS, ADDING THE PENNANT AT THE MASTHEAD IN THEIR PLACE. IT WAS OFFICIALLY RELEASED IN MARCH 1944. (U.S. NAVY, NARA)

Leonard Roy Harmon, a posthumous recipient of the Navy Cross, was born on January 21, 1917, in Cuero, Texas. He also holds the honor of being the first person of African-American descent to have a US Navy ship named after them.

Harmon graduated from Daule High School and during the Great Depression he worked on various house and grounds chores at the historic William Frobese home in Cuero. On June 10, 1939, Harmon enlisted in the United States Navy in Houston and trained at Norfolk, Virginia. He reported to the USS San Francisco for duty on October 28, 1939.

On board the cruiser, Harmon advanced to mess attendant first class. The battle of Guadalcanal began on November 12, 1942, with a Japanese aerial assault on American warships protecting transports that were unloading reinforcements for the Marines on the island. A damaged Japanese plane deliberately crashed into the cruiser's radar and fire-control station, killing or injuring fifty men.

The next day, the San Francisco was raked by enemy gunfire that killed nearly every officer on the bridge. Disregarding his own safety, Harmon helped evacuate the wounded to a dressing station. He was killed while shielding a wounded shipmate from gunfire. For "extraordinary heroism," he was posthumously awarded the Navy Cross. On May 21, 1943, Secretary of the Navy Frank Knox announced that a warship would be named in Harmon's honor. The USS Harmon, a destroyer escort, was launched on July 25, 1943. Other honors bestowed posthumously on Harmon include the naming and dedication of Harmon Hall, bachelor enlisted quarters at the United States Naval Air Station, North Island, California, in 1975 and the placing of a state historical marker at Cuero Municipal Park in 1977. ★

WORLD WAR II'S "BUFFALO SOLDIERS":

THE 92ND INFANTRY DIVISION. BY: BILL CHAMBRÉS

The 92nd Infantry Division, a military unit of approximately fifteen thousand officers and men, was one of only two all-black divisions to fight in the United States Army in World War I and World War II.

The 92nd Division was organized in October 1917 at Camp Funston, Kansas, and included black soldiers from across the United States. Before leaving for France in 1918, it received the name "Buffalo Soldier Division" as a tribute to the four Buffalo soldier regiments that fought in the regular U.S. Army in the nineteenth and early twentieth centuries.

After the United States entered World War II, the 92nd Infantry was reactivated on October 15, 1942, and trained at Fort Huachuca, Arizona, with the 93rd Infantry, the other all-black division. After that training was completed, the 92nd was deployed to Italy while its counterpart was sent to the South Pacific. On July 30, 1944, the first units of the 92nd arrived in Naples, Italy, and by September 22, the entire division was stationed in the Po Valley in North Italy. Assigned to the U.S. Fifth Army, the 92nd Division also included the 442nd Regimental Combat Team, the all-Japanese-American (Nisei) unit that both suffered some of the heaviest casualties of the war and became one of the most decorated U.S. military units. The 92nd Division returned to the United States on November 26, 1945, and was deactivated two days later on November 28, 1945.

During the fighting, First Lt. John R. Fox won the Medal of Honor for his action in the Serchio Valley on December 26, 1944, and First Lt. Vernon J. Baker won the medal for his action near Viareggio on April 5–6, 1945. Both medals were not awarded until 1997.

John Robert Fox (May 18, 1915 – December 26, 1944) was an African-American soldier killed in action when he deliberately called for artillery fire on his own position, after that position was overrun during a German attack in the vicinity of Sommocolonia in northern Italy. He posthumously received the Medal of Honor in 1997 for willingly sacrificing his life.

Fox was born in Cincinnati, Ohio, on May 18, 1915, and attended Wilberforce University, in Wilberforce, Ohio. At the university, he participated in ROTC under Aaron R. Fisher and graduated with a commission as a second lieutenant in 1940. He was 29 years old when he called for that artillery fire on his own position the day after Christmas in 1944, for which he was posthumously awarded the Distinguished Service Cross in 1982. More than fifty years after his death, Fox was awarded the Medal of Honor. He is buried in Colebrook Cemetery in Whitman, Massachusetts.

In the early 1990s, it was determined that African-American soldiers had been denied consideration for the Medal of Honor because of their race. After a review, seven African-American soldiers, including 1st Lieutenant Fox, had their medals upgraded in January 1997 to the Medal of Honor.

Vernon Joseph Baker (December 17, 1919 – July 13, 2010) was a United States Army officer in the 92nd Infantry Division who was awarded the Medal of Honor for his actions on April 5–6, 1945, near Viareggio, Italy.

Baker was born on December 17, 1919, in Cheyenne, Wyoming, he was the youngest of three children. After his parents died in a car accident when he was four, he and his two sisters were raised by their paternal grandparents.

He attempted to enlist in April 1941 but was turned away, the recruiter stating, "We don't have any quotas for you people." Baker tried again weeks later with a different recruiter and was accepted. He requested to become a quartermaster but was assigned instead to the infantry.

Baker entered the Army on June 26, 1941, six months prior to the U.S. entry into World War II. He went through training at Camp Wolters, Texas, and after completing Officer Candidate School was commissioned as a second lieutenant on January 11, 1943. In June 1944, Baker was sent to Italy with the all-black 92nd Infantry Division. He was wounded in the arm in October of that year, hospitalized near Pisa, and in December rejoined his unit in reserve along the Gothic Line.

In early spring 1945, his unit was pulled from reserve status and ordered into combat. On the morning of April 5, Baker participated in an attack on the German stronghold of Castle Aghinolfi. During the assault, Baker led his heavy weapons platoon through German army defenses to within sight of the castle, personally destroying a machine gun position, two observation posts, two bunkers, and a network of German telephone lines along the way. It was for these and other actions, including leading a battalion advance under heavy fire, that he was later awarded the Medal of Honor

Baker was the only black American World War II veteran of the seven belatedly awarded the Medal of Honor who was still living when it was bestowed upon him by President Bill Clinton in 1997. He died in 2010 at the age of 90.

By the end of the Italian Campaign, which began in 1943 and ended with the surrender of the German Armed Forces in May 1945, a bond was built between the soldiers of the 92nd Division and the Italian population. The Italians still remember the black GIs of the 92nd as liberators and good Samaritans. ★

REPRODUCTION NO. 208-AA49E-1-13; "NEGRO 'DOUGHFOOTS' OF THE 92ND INFANTRY ('BUFFALO') DIVISION PURSUE THE RETREATING GERMANS THROUGH THE PO VALLEY. GERMAN FORCES IN ITALY HAVE SINCE CAPITULATED UNCONDITIONALLY." CA. MAY 1945. NATIONAL ARCHIVES AND RECORDS ADMINISTRATION.

JOHN FOX POSTHUMOUSLY RECEIVED THE MEDAL OF HONOR IN 1997 FOR ACTIONS DURING WORLD WAR II. THE 366TH INFANTRY REGIMENT YEARBOOK FOR 1941.

VERNON BAKER, US ARMY, WORLD WAR II MEDAL OF HONOR RECIPIENT. WWW.HOMEOFHEROES.COM

AFRICAN-AMERICAN TROOPS AND THE 'ALCAN' HIGHWAY

BY: BILL CHAMBRÉS

During World War II, African-American troops fought and served in every theater of the war. Europe and the Pacific are the most known areas but there was another lesser-known territory where they served.

At the time of the war, Alaska, now the 49th and largest state in the nation, was a territory purchased from the Russian Empire in 1867 for $7.2 million, or approximately two cents per acre. Alaska gained its rights as an organized incorporated territory of the United States in 1912. Once drawn into World War II, the U.S. government worried that Japan would follow the destruction of the U.S. Pacific fleet in Hawaii with an invasion of Alaska. Within a few weeks of the Pearl Harbor attack, President Franklin D. Roosevelt decided that plans for a highway to Alaska deserved re-examination.

This resolution became the first step in what one army colonel characterized as the 'biggest and hardest job since the Panama Canal.' Despite obstacles that might have doomed the project had it been undertaken in peacetime, in less than nine months a rapidly marshaled force of almost 16,000 soldiers and civilians forged 1,422 miles of roadway from Dawson Creek, British Columbia, to

CATERPILLAR TRACTOR CUTTING A ROAD THROUGH THE FOREST FOR THE ALCAN HIGHWAY. 1942. LIBRARY OF CONGRESS REPRODUCTION NO. LC-USW33-000945-ZC.

BRIDGE FOR THE ALCAN HIGHWAY CONSTRUCTION BUILT OVER A TRIBUTARY OF THE PEACE RIVER. 1942. LIBRARY OF CONGRESS REPRODUCTION NO. LC-USW33-000946-ZC.

Delta Junction, Alaska. There the road joined the pre-existing Richardson Highway (which originally began as a trail for gold stampeders in 1898) for the remaining 98 miles to Fairbanks. The Highway was engineered to be built through some of the roughest imaginable terrain and under severe inclement weather conditions.

Included in the building of the highway was the Canadian Oil (CANOL) Project, a refinery and pipeline system that stretched across northwest Canada and Alaska, built concurrently at the behest of the War Department to satisfy the petroleum needs of the highway, and the Northwest Staging Route, a string of small landing fields established earlier across western Canada for military use. It was the most expensive construction project of the war and the most criticized. Politicians on both sides of the Canada-U.S. border questioned the highway's usefulness, and at least one politician — U.S. Senator Harry S Truman — saw his career boosted by raising doubts about this vast military enterprise.

While most U.S. troops were being utilized in the European and Pacific theaters, there were few left for such a huge project. Therefore, the work fell to troops who were underutilized. In this case, these were the units of the African-American engineer regiments. In 1942, the Army Corps of Engineers

else, they also had to contend with relentless racism. The Army was still segregated, and black units were led by white officers. As late as 1936, a manpower assessment produced at the Army War College described black soldiers as shiftless, dishonest, and lazy. "Say what you will," the report declared, "the American Negro is still a primitive human being." It was a view the Army as a whole embraced. The officers in charge were usually Southerners who supposedly "understood" blacks but in fact disparaged and despised them. Senior commanders of the road-building effort, one of them the son of a Confederate general, declared that blacks (often they called them something else) might be able to wield picks and shovels but not the heavy equipment the job required.

TRUCKS LOADING UP AT THE GRAVEL DUMP. MOST OF THE GRAVEL USED FOR SURFACING ALONG THE ALCAN HIGHWAY WAS OBTAINED FROM GLACIAL DEPOSITS FOUND ALONGSIDE THE ROADWAY. 1942. LIBRARY OF CONGRESS REPRODUCTION NO. LC-USW33-000953-ZC.

ARMY TRUCKS ALONG THE ALCAN HIGHWAY FORM STIFF COMPETITION FOR THE LOCAL DOGSLED TRANSPORTATION. 1942. LIBRARY OF CONGRESS REPRODUCTION NO. LC-USW33-000949-ZC.V

assigned more than 10,000 men to build the Alaska Canada Military Highway. About a third (3,695) were black soldiers. They were members of three predominantly African American Engineer General Service Regiments: the 93th, 95th and 97th. Many of the black soldiers hailed from the South and had never seen snow, much less temperatures that sometimes dropped to minus 50. However, despite this and other hardships, they played a vital role in assuring the roadwork was completed on schedule.

Though the black soldiers had to face the vicious cold, heat, mosquitoes, and mud like everyone

So when they were issued heavy equipment, black units sometimes received vehicles otherwise headed for the scrapheap. And sometimes they lost even that to white units whose equipment was delayed or damaged.

The men were soon to be tested at the bridge project over the Sikanni Chief, a fast-flowing river through a gorge 300 feet wide in the mountains of British Columbia. By working three days straight, at times by the light of their truck headlights, the men felled trees, squared timbers, assembled trestles, and waded chest deep into the ice-cold river to float them into position. They cut and assembled wood to form the bridge's decking and installed heavy timber cribs to protect its footings from ice and driftwood. The 300-foot bridge was completed in 72-hours.

A photograph of this bridge, with a caption saying who built it, appeared in Time magazine in August 1942, and the unit had won a reputation on the ground as fast workers who produced sturdy bridges under highly adverse conditions while operating their heavy equipment in the Alcan's cold, heat, and mud.

In October of that year, two crews, one moving north and one moving south, completed the road's last link.

The story captured the public's imagination. The Engineering News Record called it "two races, working together to build a lifeline to Alaska's beleaguered defenders amidst the most spectacularly rugged terrain and horrendous weather conditions imaginable." The Army even promoted the story in Yank, its magazine for the troops.

When the highway was officially dedicated on November 21, 1942, Corporal Sims, Private Jalufka, and two other soldiers, one black and one white, were there to hold the ceremonial ribbon.

Six years later, President Harry S. Truman ordered the

EDMONTON (VICINITY), CANADA. SUPPLIES FOR BUILDING THE ALCAN HIGHWAY BEING TRANSPORTED STERN-WHEELER. 1942. LIBRARY OF CONGRESS REPRODUCTION NO. LC-USW33-000931-ZC.

OPENING CEREMONIES OF THE ALCAN HIGHWAY AT SOLDIERS' SUMMIT, A STRETCH OF HIGHWAY 1500 FEET ABOVE THE WIDE SWATH OF KLUANE LAKE, WHICH IS APPROXIMATELY 100 MILES EAST OF THE ALASKA-YUKON INTERNATIONAL BOUNDARY. 1949. LIBRARY OF CONGRESS REPRODUCTION NO. LC-USW33-000932-ZC.

Later, the New York Times reported what happened when they "met head-on in the spruce forests of the Yukon Territory."

"Corporal Refines Sims Jr., a Negro from Philadelphia, was driving south with a bulldozer when he saw trees starting to topple over on him," the account said. "Slamming his big vehicle into reverse, he backed out just as another bulldozer, driven by Private Alfred Jalufka of Kennedy, Texas, broke through the underbrush." The article continued, "Immediately after this Yukon version of driving the golden spike, Sims and Jalufka turned their bulldozers around and began widening the opening."

Army desegregated, and many historians cite the Alcan experience as helping make that possible. On its Web site, the Federal Highway Administration calls the Alcan "the road to civil rights."

*For an informative account see Heath Twichell's Northwest Epic (St. Martin's Press, 1992). Twichell's father, Colonel Heath Twichell Sr., was a commander assigned to a black unit working on the project. ★

TUSKEGEE AIRMEN
99TH PURSUIT SQUADRON BY: BILL CHAMBRÉS

Less than a year before the attack on Pearl Harbor, on January 16, 1941, the War Department announced the formation of the 99th Pursuit Squadron, an African-American unit, and the Tuskegee Institute training program. On March 7, 1942, exactly three months after the attack, the first graduating class of the Air Corps Advanced Flying School at Tuskegee Field included Colonel (later General) Benjamin O. Davis, Jr. He became the commanding officer of the 99th Fighter Squadron and later the 332d Fighter Group. These units were unique in United States military history because all personnel were African American.

The 99th Fighter Squadron was shipped to North Africa in April 1943 and flew its first combat mission against the island of Pantelleria on June 2, 1943. Captain Charles B. Hall became the first African-American pilot to shoot down an enemy aircraft. Later, the squadron, operating from its base in North Africa, supported the invasion of Italy and participated in the air battle against Sicily. After serving in North Africa, the 99th moved to Sicily and the mainland of Italy to support Allied campaigns there. It was later assigned to the 332nd Fighter Group, which had three other squadrons, and together they later took part in raids on Germany and other parts of central Europe.

Although the Airmen flew courageously and well, it was as bomber escorts on missions deep into Germany and surrounding areas that they really made a name for themselves. They gained a widespread reputation for staying with the bombers and successfully protecting them during their dangerous missions. Other fighter squadrons were known to be more interested in going after enemy aircraft for an aerial victory, but the Tuskegee Airmen followed their strict orders to stay with the bombers and gained notoriety for their success at protecting these aircraft from being shot down.

When the pilots of the 332nd Fighter Group painted the tails of their P-47s (and later P-51s) red, the nickname "Red Tails" was coined. The red markings that distinguished the Tuskegee Airmen included red bands on the noses of P-51s as well as a red rudder; the P-51B and D Mustangs flew with similar color schemes with red propeller spinners, yellow wing bands, and all-red tail surfaces.

The 332d Fighter Group flew more than 3,000 missions in Europe and destroyed almost 300 enemy planes. Eighty-eight of the group's pilots received the Distinguished Flying Cross, proving their test by fire a success. ★

CAPTS. LEMUEL R. CUSTIS AND CHARLES B. HALL, OF THE ALL-AFRICAN-AMERICAN 99TH FIGHTER SQUADRON, ON LEAVE IN NEW YORK CITY IN JUNE, 1944. WHILE IN ACTION IN NORTH AFRICA AND ITALY, THEY FLEW OVER 3,000 SORTIES IN ONE YEAR, AS BOMBING ESCORT, DIVE BOMBING, BEACHHEAD PATROL, OR STRAFING, AND SHOT DOWN 17 PLANES. (NARA)

REPRODUCTION NO. 80-G-54413; "MEMBERS OF THE 99TH FIGHTER SQUADRON OF THE ARMY AIR FORCES, FAMOUS ALL-NEGRO OUTFIT, WHO ARE RAPIDLY MAKING THEMSELVES FEARED BY ENEMY PILOTS, POSE FOR A PICTURE AT THE ANZIO BEACHHEAD. IN THE FOREGROUND, HEAD BARED, IS 1ST LT. ANDREW LANE." CA. FEBRUARY 1944. NATIONAL ARCHIVES AND RECORDS ADMINISTRATION.

FROM MONTFORD POINT TO IWO JIMA:

ONE PATH FOR AFRICAN AMERICAN MARINES IN WWII

BY: BILL CHAMBRÉS

In 1941, President Franklin D. Roosevelt ordered the Marine Corps to accept African Americans. It was the last military branch to do so, and recruiting began on June 1, 1942, albeit reluctantly.

Black Marines received basic training at Camp Gilbert H. Johnson at Montford Point, North Carolina, a satellite camp of Marine Corps Base Camp Lejeune. Camp Johnson was home to the Marine Corps Combat Service Support Schools (MCCSSS), where various support military occupational specialties such as administration, supply, logistics, finance, and motor transport maintenance were trained.

The camp was in an area of swamps and flooded forests, and conditions could be harsh, but the treatment from their fellow Marines could be even harsher. Black Marines were not allowed to enter Camp Lejeune unless accompanied by a white officer, could not eat until the white Marines had finished, and were routinely passed over for promotions.

Of the nearly 21,609 African Americans in the Marines who trained at Montford Point, 75 percent had been to college. Though more than 13,000 went overseas, none saw combat until Saipan. There, as elsewhere, black Marines staffed depot and ammunition companies and transported weapons and munitions, medical supplies, and food and water from ship to shore—6,000 tons per day.

Though the loaders toiled in punishing heat among falling shells and the hammering of Nambu machine guns, they would not see action officially until casualties cut deeply into other fighting forces. With no reserves left, the Montford Point Marines were sent to the front. The move stunned white Marines until they saw that a man's color didn't matter when he stood his ground and fought.

"One of the bravest sights I've seen was on Iwo Jima where a black driver of a "duck," time and time again delivered much needed ammunition."

One of those men was orderly Kenneth Tibbs, of Columbus, Ohio. He was killed by an artillery round soon after landing on Saipan, the first African-American Marine to die in the war. Time magazine took note and wrote, "Negro Marines, under fire for the first time, have rated a universal 4.0 on Saipan."

Kenneth Rollock, from Harlem, New York, joined despite knowing that "In the Navy, all the blacks were either cooks, busboys, or servants. . . . If I was going to fight for this country, I wasn't going to fight by cooking." Rollock got his chance when the 3rd Ammunition Company filled a gap in the lines. "About a quarter mile from the beach, they came out screaming, and we just opened up. Anything moving we shot at." Rollock said later he would never forget those sounds.

On Iwo Jima, elements of the 8th Marine Ammunition Company and the 36th Marine Depot Companies landed on D-Day, February 19, 1945, braving Japanese fire as they struggled in the volcanic sand to unload and stockpile ammunition and other supplies to move inland. While they were not supposed to take part in combat, black Marines played a significant role in defeating the attackers. Eleven black enlisted Marines and one of the white officers were wounded, two of the enlisted men fatally. Under enemy fire they piloted amphibious trucks during perilous shore landings, unloaded and shuttled ammunition to the front lines, helped bury the dead, and weathered Japanese onslaughts even after the island had been declared secure.

Company—Privates James M. Whitlock and James Davis—earned the Bronze Star for their heroism. Six Marines were wounded, two fatally. The African-American companies at Iwo Jima shared in the Navy Unit Citation awarded to the support units of V Amphibious Corps.

In 1998, Parris Island drum major Staff Sgt. Vernon Harris composed the music for "I'll Take the Marines" to accompany lyrics written by Montford Marine LaSalle Vaughn. Harris noted, "If African Americans at that time could go through the rigorous training of Marines when it was segregated. . .and still be proud Marines. . . . it encourages all Marines to look forward and recognize our progress," ★

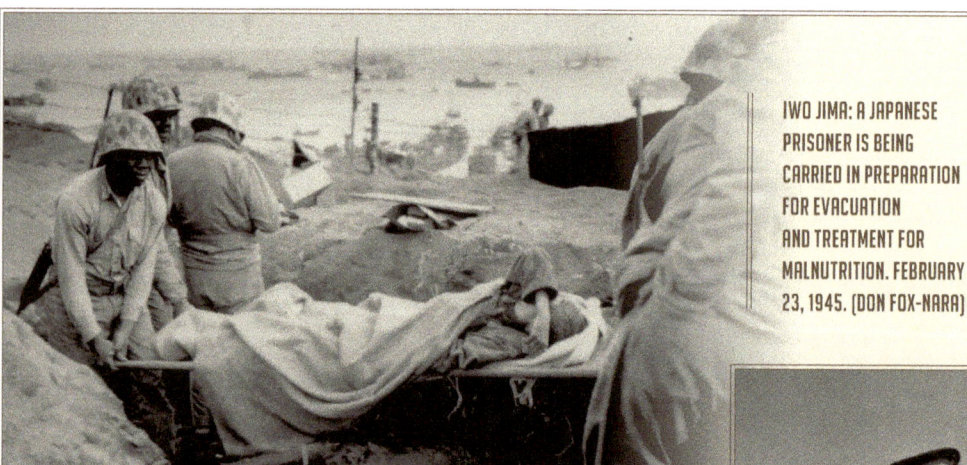

IWO JIMA: A JAPANESE PRISONER IS BEING CARRIED IN PREPARATION FOR EVACUATION AND TREATMENT FOR MALNUTRITION. FEBRUARY 23, 1945. (DON FOX-NARA)

Thousands more helped fashion the airstrips from which U.S. B-29 aircrafts could launch and return from air assaults on Tokyo, about 760 miles northwest. Hosting that air base was Iwo Jima's primary strategic importance. Eyewitness Jim Rundles wrote: "One of the bravest sights I've seen was on Iwo Jima where a black driver of a "duck," time and time again delivered much needed ammunition."

During the early morning of March 26, ten days after Iwo Jima was declared secure, the Japanese made a final attack. The black Marines helped stop the enemy in a confused struggle during darkness and two members of the 36th

PUBLICITY PHOTO WORK WOTH SGT. LUCIOUS A. WILSON, PHOTOGRAPHER, CPL. EDWIN K. ANDERSON, AND FORMER CORRESPONDEDNT FOR NEW YORK AMSTERDAM NEWS SGT. WILSON. (NARA)

Want to **WRITE A BOOK,** but don't know **WHERE TO START?**

Speak with a 30+ YEAR book publishing veteran today.

Get answers TODAY! Call **717.731.1405**

ISBN/Bar Codes	Text Design
Book Coach	Editing
Manuscript Evaluations	Nationwide Distribution
Cover Design	Printing

www.OrisonPublishers.com

www.ingramcontent.com/pod-product-compliance
Lightning Source LLC
Chambersburg PA
CBHW051403110526
44592CB00023B/2941